The New Method Of Selling

"Sales Mastery in the Age of Expert Consumers"

By

Edwin D. Richards

Table Of Contents

Introduction

Welcome to a transformative journey through the world of sales. In these pages, we'll explore not just the techniques but also the underlying principles and strategies that define successful salesmanship. Each chapter is a stepping stone, designed to unravel the complexities, myths, and challenges salespeople encounter daily.

Chapter by chapter, we'll dive deep into the heart of sales, starting with identifying and understanding the biggest challenges faced in the industry. Then, we'll debunk common misconceptions, paving the way for a clearer understanding of what truly works. From breaking through the gatekeeper's barriers to fostering a customer-centric approach, we'll equip you with the tools to navigate the intricacies of the sales process.

Communication is at the core of successful salesmanship. Chapters on the power of voice, active listening, and the art of questioning will refine your communication skills, empowering you to engage and understand your customers more effectively. But it doesn't stop there—this book takes you through the stages of engagement, transition, and commitment, providing a roadmap to nurture relationships and drive results.

Ultimately, the goal is not just to sell but to cultivate enduring business relationships. By the end of this journey, you'll be equipped with insights and strategies to elevate your sales approach and take your business relationship to the next level. So, let's embark together on this enlightening expedition into the realm of successful salesmanship.

Chapter One

Identifying the Key Challenges in Sales

Every sales agent aspires to conclude their month on a cheerful note celebrating their successes. But tragically, for most salespeople, it ends with the sadness of missed objectives. Sales representatives are often afflicted by challenges that negatively impact their sales outcomes.

The problem is that most sales personnel ignore these obstacles and continue selling, resulting in the same unsatisfactory sales results month after month. When faced with a challenge, search for a way, not a way out.

Common Sales Challenges and Their Solutions

No one is immune to challenges, not even the best salespeople. However, they handle the sales issues rather than dismissing them. Accept the trials so that you may enjoy the pleasure of triumph.

Here are the most typical issues that most sales representatives experience, as well as answers to them;

Sales Challenge 1 – Competing with Competitors.

The market has become a battleground where firms do whatever it takes to overcome their rivals. Competitors are experimenting with numerous ways to entice clients, ranging from cutting rates to giving freebies.

Potential purchasers identify such points and use them as a shield to negotiate a lower price for the goods. Most salespeople get to hear statements like "The [X competitor] is offering a product at a much lower price" or "The [Y competitor] is offering a free four-month subscription to their service."

When confronted with such situations, most sellers either go blank or make rash decisions that jeopardize their revenues.

Solution:

• After doing an in-depth competition study, map out your rivals' strengths and shortcomings.

• Find out how you are better than your competition and explain it to your prospective consumers.

• Share case studies and testimonials of satisfied customers who selected you over the rivals.

Sales Challenge 2 – Insufficient Selling Time

Sales salespeople have a large to-do list. From gathering facts about the possible customer to crafting sales letters as well as updating records, there is a lot a sales agent must do in a day. Furthermore, if things aren't ordered, more time is spent looking for information. Sales representatives do not have enough time to strategize and sell. Salespeople spend almost a third of their time (35.2%) selling.

Solution:

• Use an automation tool to put most of your duties on autopilot.

• Use technologies that provide profile enrichment capabilities to automatically get crucial information about your prospects.

• Instead of writing each email from scratch, create and reuse email templates.

• Using sales reports, keep track of your sales efforts and prioritize your tasks for the week.

• Instead of utilizing diaries and notebooks, choose a platform to store all of your client information.

Sales Challenge 3 – No Reaction from the Prospect

Most prospects quit responding after a few first contacts. This silence demotivates many sales representatives. They forsake the lead and shift their attention to another possibility. As a result, the majority of leads are not converted.

Solution:

• Follow up continuously without giving up. You may utilize solutions that enable you to design email and text sequences for automating the follow-up.

• To enhance your response rate, use intriguing email subject lines and content.

• Attempt to contact someone else at the prospect's company.

• Connect with the prospect at various hours. Explore the optimal time to call or send emails to the prospect.

• Use alternative methods aside from calls and emails to communicate with your prospects like text messaging and social media sites.

Sales Challenge 4 – Prospects' hesitation during the negotiation

The majority of transactions are lost at the negotiating stage of the sales process. Several prospects are hesitant to make concessions or establish common ground. Furthermore, the prospect's hesitancy irritates the salespeople, who end up releasing their frustration unpleasantly.

Solution:

• Maintain your cool throughout the discussion and ponder before responding to a customer's complaint.

• Research and explore numerous negotiating methods to deal with resistant prospects.

• Identify the prospects' pressure points and help them envision the implications of not addressing the issue right now.

• To begin, set a high price. Then charge a cheap fee for a restricted set of features. While the prospect is swinging between two offers, make the genuine offering.

Sales Challenge 5 – Unable to deal with criticism or rejection

Most salespeople cannot hear "NO" and cannot take criticism. They get discouraged. This even impacts their next transaction as they cannot concentrate on communication due to the disappointment from the rejection or criticism they experience.

Solution:

• Practice and prepare a nice reaction whenever you receive a no.

• Don't let your emotions take over; instead, build on your EQ (Emotional Intelligence).

• Ask your senior to arrange a mock call session to train you to manage rejection on sales calls.

• Create a lot of possibilities for yourself so that few rejections don't damage your aim.

Sales Challenge 6 – Sales training

Most firms establish high expectations but fail to give sufficient training to sales representatives for dealing with today's sophisticated customers. The biggest reason for poor sales productivity is a lack of training. The majority of the salespeople are having difficulty hitting their sales targets.

Solution:

• Find the areas where training is necessary and urge management to invest in training.

• Learn from industry professionals by attending live webinars.

• Ask top sales professionals to offer frequent performance comments.

Sales Challenge 7 – Unable to monitor deals

The sales pipeline could have several transactions. Unfortunately, the majority of them get blocked for an extended period at some point in the sales funnel and eventually fall through the cracks. Several salespeople lack insight into their sales pipeline, which causes them to miss out on numerous possibilities.

Solution:

• Use the finest CRM available. It will...

• Give you full insight into each step of the sales funnel.

• Allow you to categorize and prioritize high-value transactions to follow their development.

• Keep you up to date on all aspects of the transaction.

Sales Challenge 8 – Insufficient time to engage in prospecting.

Prospecting is a highly crucial step in the sales process. However, most sales professionals find it tough to spend time prospecting.

Making cold calls consistently will familiarize you with several profitable chances. So do not neglect this vital sales activity.

Solution:

• Set up a certain period each day to conduct cold calls.

• Use a power dialer to save time and boost efficiency.

• Do not disregard cold calling for any other job.

Sales Challenge 9 – Unable to respond to prospect queries

Modern customers are very intelligent and well-informed. They are updated with the current industry trends and popular technology. As a result, they tend to ask a lot of questions. Most of the time, salespeople go blank and are unable to answer these queries. Do you have this challenge? If so, the following actions are required of you.

Solution:

• First and foremost, ensure that you are well-versed about the product.

• Make a list of frequently asked questions and prepare for them.

• Have a simulated phone session with your senior

Chapter Two

Misconceptions Versus Truths in Sales Practices

When individuals hear the term "sales," they may think of demanding revenue goals, constant calls, and long hours. While certain sales professions might be hard, this one-sided impression takes away from the reality that the area of sales is frequently a rewarding career option.

Depending on where you work, your sales career will most likely provide you with a flexible work schedule, the opportunity to broaden your talents, and a high salary potential. The following are ten popular sales myths.

1. Sales Is 'Just A Job'

The most common mistake about sales is that it is just "a job." Sales is, of course, a profession, but it is also a mindset, a way of thinking about and doing things. It's critical to grasp the basic value of sales skills, the power of influence, how habits shape our actions, and what it takes to build a solid relationship with the people you work with, especially as a new grad. By recognizing and pressing these levers,

15

professionals may open doors and generate a powerful impact—no sales degree or special job title is necessary!

2. Sales Is An Unstable Career Path

Sales jobs are sometimes linked with long hours, endless travel, and unstable wages, but this is no longer the case. Salespeople may work reasonably regular hours and earn stable wages with sufficient training and the correct corporate culture. And, in the post-COVID-19 world, many of the tasks that salesmen used to do in person are now completed online. Sales is a more secure job than fresh graduates may believe, and it provides a solid business foundation that may be transferred to other firms or positions in the future.

3. Only Sales Experience Can Help With Sales

A prevalent misperception is that working in sales can only assist you with one career—sales. On the contrary, everything in today's corporate world is about selling. Starting with a sales job is like getting a crash lesson in soft skills, which will give you a leg up in any business profession and pretty much any flexible role inside the gig economy—whether you want to try your hand as a creator, solo consultant, entrepreneur, or anything else. It certainly is freeing. Sales is at the very core of my profession as a multi-business founder and CEO and I enjoy it. Being excellent at it seems like a particular power. As an entrepreneur, you have to sell so many people on your concept, from your investors to first customers to new staff.

4. Selling Is Bad

Selling something is not a terrible thing. Appropriately selling something helps the salesman to be "of service" to the prospective customer. Many people regard sales as a negative, but when you genuinely work to find a need that the prospective customer has, I would argue that you must inform the individual about your answer. In this approach, you might be "of service" by helping the individual solve an issue. If they don't have an issue or a need for what you are offering, then move on. Sales is a terrific profession and a great experience when you discover a product or service that satisfies a market demand. Otherwise, the salesman is swimming upstream in a very unpleasant and unfulfilling manner, likely contributing to many of the bad conceptions of selling.

5. Sales Isn't a Realistic Career Option

With so many individuals attempting to sell everything and social media influencers around every corner, everyone is suffering from information and content overload. It has perpetuated the misconception that salesmen don't have a "real job" and aren't interested in assisting you. Sales is a genuine and very difficult job option. It takes someone honest, focused on adding value, and interested in helping others. It's one thing to simply seal a sale, but it's another to be able to care about the empowerment of the customer. The most effective salesmen recognize that assisting others is the most essential job of all.

6. The Internet Has Rendered Sales Obsolete

I've heard from college students and new college graduates that sales occupations are dead today with the development of the internet and social media. But that's so far from the reality. Law businesses, professional service organizations, medical facilities, PR and marketing agencies, etc., all need business development experts to expand and prosper. Cold calling, cold emailing, and connection building are essential to the success of any firm.

7. Salespeople are uninterested in assisting others.

Contrary to common belief, sales do not have to be "salesy" and you cannot be like that if you want to complete a transaction. We are no longer in the 1990s when invasive telemarketing earned our industry a poor name. Helping consumers discover answers to their issues is at the heart of modern sales. It's not about deceiving people into purchasing something they don't need. And sales don't even have to be outbound, since today's clients want to be seeking for assistance on their own. Here's a simple example to help you adjust your viewpoint on it: When you go to a job interview, what you are doing is attempting to market your talent to the company that is seeking it. Both of you need it. So fundamentally, it's about proving value.

8. Sales Makes People Uncomfortable

Prospective graduates who are wondering about their future employment may believe sales is awful and that individuals in sales are not being acknowledged because they are too demanding. They may assume they have to sell to their family and friends, and that might seem weird. As someone who came from a clinical background and moved into sales, I will tell you that you are mistaken. We are selling and being marketed to every single day, numerous times a day. You don't have to consider sales to be an "uncomfortable" professional path if you're not passionate about the product or service you're selling.

9. It Doesn't Matter What You Sell

Because it is consistent, sales is always a fantastic area to enter into. There must be a salesperson for every service or product. Those who excel at it may earn a fortune. The misunderstanding is that it doesn't matter what you sell. It is the one thing that does matter. Every salesman must believe in what they are selling. They understand that their product or service will make the lives of others simpler. This is the mark of a genuine salesman. The second prevalent problem is many, especially young individuals, assume they don't need to prepare to sell. They assume they can simply go over the technicalities and the transaction occurs. A great salesman is well-versed in their product or service and can explain how it may benefit the other person.

10. Sales are shady.

I suppose most people regard sales as a variant of the used car salesperson, attempting to pass something off on an unknowing receiver. The fact is that sales are merely the medium through which our modern society was constructed, and those who master the craft may find work in nearly any field. Sales transcends any one specialty or industry, and when you are a master of the trade, you may begin to pick and choose where and for whom you work. Very few skill sets offer you that kind of flexibility or choice. There is a reason why the greatest salesmen are paid on commission rather than salary and seldom attend local meetings.

Chapter Three
Navigating Access Barriers

The despised gatekeeper. You know, the secretary or assistant who shields prospects from cold calls?

They perform their job so effectively that getting past them is one of the most typical obstacles in B2B sales. So, how do you get past the guard?

While there is no secret recipe, there are various tactics you may use to increase your chances of success. This chapter will go over them, as well as:

- Meaning of gatekeeping in B2B sales
- Getting past the gatekeeper scripts

What exactly is a gatekeeper?

A gatekeeper in B2B sales is somebody who takes calls on behalf of a corporation or decision-maker. They are generally the first point of contact for companies and include receptionists, personal assistants, secretaries or spouses and family. When a gatekeeper is engaged, you must first persuade them that your call is critical to the company.

Don't be intimidated. Sometimes it's not only an issue of getting past the gatekeeper but establishing a strong enough first impression that they become your buddy. How can you achieve this while still dealing with gatekeeping sales objections?

Here are the top 11 simple tactics that have been proven to work:

1. Make use of the prospect's cellphone number.

Calling your prospect's mobile phone number is the simplest and most effective approach to get past the gatekeeper. It is more efficient than using straight dials.

Direct dials are phone numbers that are allocated to a specific employee. If your prospect is out of the office or not at their desk, the phone might be answered by an assistant or not answered at all.

2. Do your research

The answer to getting past the gatekeeper in sales is to study your prospect and their gatekeeper. This seems like a lot of labor, but there's a rationale behind this sales tactic:

When you mention the gatekeeper in passing, you're expressing interest in them as more than a job title and engaging on a human-to-human basis. You don't want to come off as weird, so don't tell them all you know about them. Incorporate your expertise into the discourse to establish credibility and demonstrate that you are paying attention.

3. No matter what, don't be rude.

The gatekeeper's job, like cold calling, requires communicating with people who aren't usually pleasant. Begin your friendship with them by being polite and courteous. This will considerably boost your chances of getting a meeting with your target prospect.

4. Demonstrate respect

Treating gatekeepers with respect goes hand in hand with being courteous. They are an important element of the B2B organization you're contacting and often have clout with your sales prospect.

To get past gatekeepers, explain how you respect their time and appreciate their supporting you. In the end, being courteous and pleasant will go far further for you than requesting to talk to their supervisor.

5. Don't try to sell to the gatekeeper.

While being courteous and polite might help you build relationships with gatekeepers, you should avoid pitching to them. They may be interested in what you're offering and can bring you in touch with a prospect, but they will not be engaged in the sales process or purchase decision. Plus, they won't have the same pain problems as the decision maker in the company, therefore they could not see the entire breadth of your product or service.

6. Maintain your cool and call on

Trying to get past the gatekeeper might be difficult. Whatever you do, keep your calm. Remember, they are merely doing their job and no amount of impatience or rage will get you past the gatekeeper and transferred to your prospect. They will not want to assist you in the future, and you will only succeed in destroying your reputation.

7. Convey confidence

Confidence is crucial, particularly when it comes to B2B prospecting. If you come off as worried or tense, a gatekeeper is more likely to provide you with a cold calling objection or reason for why their boss can't accept your call.

You have a greater probability of getting moved if you come across as essential. For a higher chance of success, maintain a comfortable and steady voice with a warm tone, and talk slowly and authoritatively.

8. Just be truthful.

Sometimes the only thing you can do is forgo the sales pitch and tell the gatekeeper why you're calling. Of course, this will not always work, but if you hilariously deliver your opening phrase, they may be inclined to let you pass.

Another method is to send a cold email to your prospect introducing yourself. Then when you phone, you may sneak past the gatekeeper by indicating you're following up on an email you sent earlier.

9. Make use of your prospect's first name.

Using a prospect's name during a cold call is smart sales psychology, as is speaking to a gatekeeper.

Using someone's name helps create trust. If you've asked to talk to your prospect by their first name, you'll come across as someone who has spoken to them previously, and you'll be more likely to get past the gatekeeper.

10. Show understanding

Showing empathy and compassion for the gatekeeper, like speaking to prospects, may go a long way. Furthermore, you might persuade the gatekeeper to open up to you by empathizing with them. This not only strengthens your friendship, but it may also provide some intriguing facts when selling to your potential customer.

11. Call again at a different time.

If you think about the optimal times to cold call, the odds are quite a few SDRs will be calling around the same time. This might leave gatekeepers upset. One method to get around this is to phone your prospect before or after usual business hours.

If you contact an executive, they tend to come earlier or remain later than other workers, so you will not only skip the gatekeeper, but you will also be able to begin a one-on-one chat with your prospect when they are a little more relaxed.

Chapter Four

Prioritizing Customer-Centric Approaches

Everything is based on experience. Make sure you get it properly. A positive customer experience makes individuals feel listened to and valued. It reduces friction, increases efficiency, and keeps a human factor.

According to research, 84% of consumers want companies to generate strong content, that engages them via narrative, delivers valuable answers, and creates engaging experiences.

Today's digital world not only focuses on but also requires customization, and firms are being established on their dedication to doing what's right for their consumers.

Many people believe that Amazon is a customer-focused firm. Because it is worldwide and enormous, it has the cash and the technical staff to fully evaluate its consumer purchasing data to target the correct messaging via the channels customers want.

Challenges and Best Practices for Creating a Customer-Centric Organization

The first stage is to get everyone on board, including leadership, marketing, sales, service, support, and finance. Then, customer-centric marketing may be accomplished by:

• Thoughtful targeting entails determining who your most probable clients are and locating them across several channels.

• Creating marketing materials for the full customer journey: People need different types of information and will be captivated by different content at various stages of the trip. For example, at the awareness stage, we typically want their attention, so commercials should be exciting, interesting, and brief; however, in the decision stage, individuals want information, want to compare items, and may like to learn more. It's one thing to have the appropriate data at the outset. However, when you collect more data and link it to the customer's profile, it directs future choices and allows you to create more targeted ads.

However, there is a caveat here that marketers should be aware of: the digital marketing industry is shifting toward less identity, less data, and more privacy (for example, the removal of third-party cookies from most browsers, or the EU's General Data Protection Regulation). Properly targeting someone requires suitable automation and optimization settings, which are not always attainable on a limited budget or with little data.

Customer-Centered Best Practices to Assist You in Achieving Your Vision

• Create a customer-focused culture. Ensure that every employee, from the CEO to the front-line employee, is obsessed with the consumer. Incorporate it into your purpose, values, and vision.

• Enhance your data. Improve the quality of your data and make it uniform and accessible to all employees. Data is often underutilized and misused. People in the company will not grasp how to interpret and utilize it correctly if it is not a tangible asset. Data may be automatically integrated using AI, for example, to resolve identities and give insights that boost customization and next-best offer campaigns. (However, keep in mind my caution above.)

• Collect client comments. It is critical to listen to what your consumers want and need by soliciting input, reading it, and incorporating it into your company strategy. Not every consumer is correct. You'll be able to tell when someone is nitpicking or worse. However, it is worthwhile to pay attention to a large number of consumers who supply the same feedback – either orally or by their actions.

• Consider the long term. A long-term consumer connection is more important than a single transaction. Develop connections with your consumers to make them feel like more than just a number. The contact you give them, the tailored offers, and your understanding of them and their preferences help you create long-term connections with them, resulting in loyalty and retention.

Chapter Five

Utilizing Vocal Power

The potential of the human voice to transmit emotion and meaning is unparalleled. We can pick up on someone's tone, intonation, and even body language when we hear their speaking voice, giving us a far fuller grasp of the message they're attempting to impart.

It's easy to lose sight of the significance of personal connection via vocal communication in today's digital world when more and more business is handled online. However, if you want to develop strong connections with your customers and establish a brand that people can relate to, you should begin by harnessing the power of your voice or by engaging a human answering service to handle your business phone calls.

Here are just a handful of the numerous reasons why the human voice remains the most potent business tool:

• **The human voice is unique.**

When you pick up the phone and call a client, you are developing a personal connection right away. You can hear their voice and they can hear yours, which builds a relationship that textual communication just cannot imitate. This personal connection enables you to establish trust and credibility with your consumers, which is necessary for any successful business partnership.

• Human Voices are Emotional

Our vocal cords can produce a broad variety of sounds and emotions, including pleasure, laughing, wrath, and melancholy. This implies that we may use our voices to express empathy and compassion as well as reasoning and reason.

How to convey messages effectively and persuasively during sales interactions.

• **Tone and Pitch:** Adjust tone for emphasis and persuasion.

The emotional weight of your message is carried by your tone. It's critical in sales to match your tone to the emotion you want to portray. For example, a passionate tone might indicate enthusiasm for a product or service, but a quiet and soothing tone can represent trust and dependability. Match your tone to the environment and the demands of your audience.

Pitch modulation aids in maintaining engagement. Pitch variation may be used to highlight crucial ideas, grab attention, and keep listeners interested. A repetitive tone of voice might dull or alienate your listeners. Experiment with various pitch levels to emphasize different components of your sales pitch and make it more dynamic and entertaining.

• **Pacing and Pausing:** Use pauses for impact and clarity.

The rate at which you talk has an effect on understanding and recall. A steady and moderate pace in sales helps your audience assimilate information properly. Rushing through might be overwhelming while speaking too slowly can lead to boredom. Adjust your tempo following the audience's reaction and the intricacy of the topic. Pauses are very effective instruments. They highlight important points, help listeners to assimilate information, and build anticipation. Pauses before and after essential information add weight and make it more remembered. Pausing also encourages engagement and clarifies concerns by inviting inquiries.

• **Confidence and Clarity:** Speak clearly and confidently to instill trust.

It is critical to have clear articulation. Use good enunciation and avoid speaking too quickly or mumbling. To ensure easy delivery, practice pronouncing difficult words or phrases. To guarantee that everyone gets your message, use straightforward language and minimize jargon.

Trust is built on confidence. Maintain proper posture, establish eye contact, and speak clearly. Believe in your product or service, and let your enthusiasm come through in your speech. Confidence spreads and might persuade prospective customers to trust what you have to offer.

The combination of these voice components may have a major influence on your capacity to convince and engage your audience in sales. Regular practice, feedback, and mindful implementation of these tactics may improve the persuasiveness and effectiveness of your sales presentations and discussions.

Chapter Six

Active Listening and Educational Absorption

In the chase of sales, it's tempting to get fixated on selling things rather than listening to your consumers. However, I have a vital insight for you that might change the way you approach sales and customer interactions. It's all about the skill of listening, particularly when it comes to your consumers. Let me give you a breakdown:

Imagine you're in a discussion where you're so focused on what you're going to say next that you lose out on the substance of what the other person is trying to express. That occurs more frequently than we'd like to acknowledge in the corporate world. We're built to think quickly, but often that speed works against us, particularly when it comes to actually knowing our consumers.

Customers are the lifeblood of every company, and if you're not listening to them, you might be losing out on important information. It's much more than simply hearing words; it's about comprehending what those words represent and comprehending the emotions and demands behind them.

Why is this so important? Let me tell you something:

To begin, diligent listening is the key to comprehending your clients' wants and preferences. It's not just about selling; it's about developing solutions that meet their needs. When you carefully listen, you may unearth ideas that can fundamentally revolutionize your sales and product development strategy.

Second, your consumers want to know that they have been heard and respected. It's human nature—we all want to be validated. Customers notice when you listen carefully. They know you care about their worries, which strengthens their bond with your business.

Third, this may come as a surprise to you, but your consumers often contain the secret to what you should be selling. Their feedback, which is distributed via multiple methods, provides you with a plethora of information about how consumers view your product. Their viewpoint may vary significantly from what you anticipate at times, and this is crucial information.

But here's the kicker: it's not just about hearing them out once. It's a constant process of learning and adjusting. The more you participate in active listening, the more you'll comprehend their shifting wants and preferences. Slowing down and listening may seem difficult in a fast-paced sales setting. But keep in mind that the benefits in terms of client retention, brand loyalty, and overall consumer pleasure are enormous.

So, here are some practical suggestions:

• Concentrate on what your consumers are saying rather than what you want to say in response.

• Pay attention to their non-verbal clues; they frequently speak louder than words.

• Allow them to freely express themselves without interfering.

• Divert your focus away from distractions; multitasking might impair comprehension.

• Confirm facts by periodically repeating what they've said; it indicates you're listening.

• Finally, put everything you've learned into practice. All of your listening will be for nothing if you don't act on it to improve their experience.

Remember, in a world where consumers have multiple alternatives, the companies that connect with them on an emotional level are the ones who succeed. So, embrace the power of listening—it could well be the key to unlocking a devoted client base and successful sales!

Chapter Seven

Strategic Questioning Techniques

The necessity of asking the appropriate questions during each sales interaction you engage with prospective customers is important to optimizing sales performance. Without asking the proper sorts of questions you may not be able to completely understand your buyer's pain points and demands, which may put you in a situation that doesn't enable you to market your goods or services in the best possible light.

As company development consultants, we understand the significance of asking the right questions at the appropriate time. Your ability to ask questions that seek out helpful information that will place you in the best position to produce and convert leads is critical to your sales success.

In this chapter, we will be using our 10+ years of experience in B2B sales, working with clients ranging from large-scale enterprises with

200-+ salespeople to micro and SME businesses to help you with the types of sales questions you should be asking, how to prepare yourself, common mistakes to avoid and overcoming some frequently encountered sales challenges.

Types of Sales Questions

In the beginning, it might be challenging to define the sort of questions you should be asking; should you be asking questions that have just one answer? Could these be queries that demand some opinion from the individual? There are several question kinds you may use, and every excellent salesman utilizes a mix of the following categories:

• Open-ended question

An open-ended question is more inviting to express opinions than a yes or no response and is designed to encourage purchasers to submit more thorough and interesting replies. These sorts of inquiries are excellent for eliciting vital information that will assist you in better understanding your buyer's wants. In a B2B sales interaction, an open-ended inquiry can be: Can you tell me more about your company's current difficulties or pain points?

• Closed-ended question

A closed-ended question, as the name suggests, is the inverse of an open-ended question. Whereas an open-ended question is meant to elicit a more thorough answer, a closed-ended question is posed when you need precise facts or specifics, such as budget allocation or deadlines. Though these questions are useful for getting clear and succinct responses, they are usually not a good idea to use at the beginning of a sales interaction since they do not inspire customers to expound on their demands.

• Probing questions

Probing inquiries are used to probe the customer to produce additional information from them. They are useful for determining a buyer's wants and motives. The goal of probing inquiries is for the customer to reveal their purchase intentions while also assisting you, the salesperson, in overcoming any sale objections they may have. Probing question kinds is useful for tailoring your approach to the buyer's demands.

• Hypothetical questions

41

Hypothetical inquiries encourage the customer to think imaginatively about their decision-making and are great for exploring possibilities, future planning, or picturing prospective advantages of your product or service with the potential client. This question type enables you to theoretically situate yourself into the client's company, allowing you to direct the discussion toward the future of your yet-to-be-established B2B partnership. As you would expect, asking enough hypothetical questions allows your prospective customer to visualize the tasks and responsibilities that you will assume after the contract is closed.

• Leading questions

Leading questions, which may be used to direct customers toward a desired conclusion or reaction, can be quite useful in a sales session. While these inquiry types are necessary, they should be used cautiously since excessive or inappropriate usage may be perceived as immoral, and some individuals may feel that they are being driven down a path rather than nurtured. Leading questions should be used to foster conversation and understanding rather than to manipulate others.

• Alternative questions

We believe in the power of questions that provide options to inspire decisiveness at Firestarter. Asking prospects if they like the red or blue choice, for example, might move the discussion along by emphasizing that the decision is in the details rather than whether to make a purchase. This method relieves decision-making stress and allows prospects to concentrate on their preferences. Remember to use these questions intelligently, finding a balance between providing options and encouraging collaboration.

The goal of the first phase of a sales interaction is to discover pain issues. This allows you to focus the discussion on those particular challenges and demonstrate how you can successfully address and fix them. Whatever form of sales question you use, it is critical to understand how, when, and why you are asking these questions. Consider your goals and the anticipated results from each interaction; avoid asking questions that provide little to no information.

Getting Ready to Ask Sales Questions

It is critical to properly understand your target market and industry, study customers and their organizations, find common pain areas and issues, and anticipate objections and concerns to effectively prepare your sales questions. By acquiring a thorough grasp of your target market and industry, you will be able to ask pertinent and informative questions that address the sector's particular requirements and trends. This information also exhibits your experience and establishes you as a reliable salesman.

Investigating buyers and their businesses may provide you with useful information that can be utilized to personalize your queries to their circumstances. This tailored approach demonstrates your real interest in their company and aids in the establishment of connection and confidence. Identifying common pain areas and obstacles with which your prospect is familiar allows you to ask tailored inquiries that address these concerns. You may show your grasp of their difficulties and position your product or service as a solution by making pain-point selling work for you.

Anticipating objections and worries ahead of time helps you to be prepared with well-crafted questions that may successfully overcome objections and address issues. This degree of preparation indicates your professionalism and aids in the development of buyer trust.

10 Must-Ask Sales Questions to Aid with Buyer Identification

As previously said, there are five sorts of sales questions to ask, each with its own set of advantages. Although there is no single "best" ratio, it is critical to concentrate on asking the correct questions at the right moment to gain information, create rapport, and successfully manage the discussion. Here are ten must-ask sales questions to understand more about your buyer:

• Could you tell me about your company?

• What problems do you want to address?

• What is preventing your team from accomplishing its objectives?

• Which areas do you think have the most potential for growth?

• Who would take part in the decision-making process?

• What is your budget for this/fixing this/purchasing this?

• What other options (internal/external) have you considered?

• How significant is this to you? Where would you place it on your priority list?

• What are the most pressing issues/areas that you believe need the greatest attention in the next 12 to 24 months?

• Do you already collaborate with any outside parties? - If so, what is your role?

These inquiries address a variety of topics, including their business's specifics, difficulties, objectives, budget, priorities, and future emphasis areas. By utilizing such questions, you can engage your buyer and understand their needs which will allow you to align your solution to their specific requirements.

Common Errors to Avoid

When conducting a sales call, the prospect of the discussion not going precisely as planned may be intimidating and frequently off-putting to sales representatives. The difference between a top-tier performance and a poor salesman is often in the manner in which they conduct their sales interactions.

• Posing slanted or prejudiced questions

Inexperienced sales representatives may fall into the trap of directing prospects down a route to a certain response; these sorts of queries are categorized as leading or biased. As previously stated, these types of questions are unethical and are frequently spotted by anyone who has ever been on a sales call; this can be quite evident among young or inexperienced sales reps. You want to come across as impartial and honest; by limiting leading or biased questions, you avoid the prospect of jumping to the wrong conclusions or answering in a way that makes them feel pressured.

• Overwhelming prospects with too many questions

We understand the significance of finding the appropriate balance when interacting with prospects; you want to acquire useful insights without overloading them with an avalanche of inquiries. By asking too many questions, you risk coming off as self-centered or even inept, since it may seem that you need a lot of attention to carry out your task. To get you started, consider these tips:

• Bring a well-thought-out list of questions. We stress the importance of extensive preparation at Firestarter to ensure that you have a clear grasp of your prospects' requirements and pain areas.

• Reduce the number of questions you ask. We instruct our salesmen at Firestarter to cross out questions that have already been answered throughout the meeting. This methodical technique guarantees that you don't ask the same questions again and over, keeping the prospect from becoming irritated or distracted.

• In the appropriate sequence, ask the right questions. The ability to ask the correct questions in the proper sequence may have a major influence on your sales performance. You may steer your prospect on a path where they persuade themselves that your solution is the best match for their requirements by carefully framing your inquiries. The purpose here is to guide the prospect on a thought-provoking journey to enable them to make an educated choice. Remember that the strength is in convincing the prospects themselves. You may convince them to feel that your answer is the best one for them by expertly asking the correct questions in the proper sequence.

• Failure to Listen Actively

Let's face it: even the most seasoned salespeople may find themselves in circumstances when they neglect to listen. But why is this happening? As humans, we are hardwired to concentrate on our ideas, views, and goals. Our minds might get so busy formulating replies and demonstrating our expertise that we accidentally fail to properly receive and comprehend what the prospect is saying.

As a result, we may miss indications, ignore small concerns, or fail to understand the prospect's genuine wants and goals. By being as present as possible and listening intently, you may assist yourself in correcting and clarifying points expressed, allowing you to offer effective follow-up questions.

Overcoming Difficulties in Sales Questioning

Meeting tough or reluctant customers is a regular difficulty that every salesman may face at some point. At Firestarter, we think that converting difficult circumstances into opportunities is critical to sales success. Using the preceding asking tactics, you will begin to notice in your sales talks which of the "gentler" inquiries assist you in negotiating your way past opposition while eventually establishing excellent rapport and building deeper partnerships.

Purchasing choices are influenced by both personal circumstances and corporate requirements. This is where not tailoring your asking skills to an individual's circumstances might slow down the sales process. Here are some Firestarter hot suggestions to help you conquer this challenge:

• **Learn about personality types** - Frameworks like DISC or the Myers-Briggs personality test are excellent methods to get acquainted with the numerous sorts of personalities. By researching each type, you may learn about general qualities, preferences, and communication styles.

• **Observe and listen** - One of the most effective ways to learn about your consumer is to just observe and listen. By utilizing open-ended inquiry tactics, you may encourage the buyer to communicate in detail about their pain areas and issues. This is an excellent way to observe their body language, tone of voice, and word choice. This may provide you with vital information about their personality type and communication style, and it allows you to alter your questioning strategies in real-time.

• **Be adaptive and flexible** - You should be prepared to accept that not everyone will react positively to your questioning style. You may change your style to match the wants of the consumer if you have an open mind and are flexible and adaptive. Your tone, tempo, and degree of information are all important factors in adjusting your sales questioning strategies.

• **Tailoring your approach** - We've discovered that during sales conversations, we can typically (and securely) assess whether the buyer is analytical, expressive, forceful, or friendly. Ask comprehensive, fact-based inquiries for analytical types that give logical reasoning and data-driven conclusions.

Expressive personalities like to tell stories or discuss situations to express their thoughts and emotions, this is where the use of open-ended questions can be utilized. Concise, straightforward queries that center on results and outcomes are well-received by assertive buyers. For amiable buyers you should employ a more empathetic and relationship-focused approach, asking questions that prioritize their feelings and opinions.

Chapter Eight

Balancing Sales Objectives

Mastering the art of time is critical in the complicated dance of sales. It is not only a matter of selling; it is also a matter of understanding when to sell and when to develop rapport and connections. The careful balance between pressing for a sale and taking a more consultative approach is critical in building long-term success. The purpose of this chapter is to go into the complexities of this balance, diving into the tactics and insights that help sales professionals navigate these seas.

• Understanding the Sales Cycle

At its foundation, sales exist on a continuum that ranges from transactional to consultative. On one end of the spectrum is the transactional approach, which is primarily concerned with completing business quickly, sometimes at the sacrifice of creating relationships. The consultative approach, on the other hand, promotes understanding customer requirements, building trust, and offering specialized solutions above fast sales.

• Detecting the Signals

The key to finding this balance is to recognize prospective customers' signs and indications. Understanding their requirements, pain areas, and willingness to buy is critical. A prospect may be eager for a speedy transaction, looking for efficiency and instant answers. Other times, they may need to take a more consultative approach, asking for direction and counsel before committing.

• Relationship Building as a Foundation

Building connections is the foundation of success in today's sales market. Even if you're looking to make a sale, spending time learning about your client's company, difficulties, and goals will pay off. Developing trust and credibility may often mean the difference between a one-time transaction and a long-term engagement.

• Developing Approaches for Various Scenarios

Approach flexibility is essential. Your capacity to adjust to changing customer demands may be hampered if your sales approach is inflexible. A seasoned sales professional understands when to take a consultative approach, cultivating the connection, and when to capitalize on momentum for a quick sale.

• Listening is a powerful tool.

The consultative method places a strong emphasis on active listening. A salesman may deliver unique solutions by first understanding the client's issues, objectives, and underlying motives. Listening carefully not only creates trust but also reveals chances where your product or service meshes perfectly with their requirements.

• Everything Depends on Timing

Timing is critical in striking a balance between pressing for a sale and building a connection. When a transaction is rushed when the customer is not ready, it may cause unhappiness and even damage the relationship. Failure to shut while the iron is hot, on the other hand, may result in squandered chances.

• Metrics Other Than Immediate Sales

It is critical to shift the emphasis from short-term sales measurements to long-term relationship-building KPIs. Client happiness, retention rates, and recommendations provide a more complete view of sales performance. A great sales approach may not always result in immediate rewards, but it may pave the way for a plethora of future chances.

In today's changing sales world, the option between pressing for a sale and nurturing relationships is not a binary one. It's an art form, a delicate dance requiring dexterity, sensitivity, and adaptation. Sales professionals may negotiate this balance by analyzing client signals, maintaining relationships, and carefully timing actions, assuring not just short-term benefits but also long-term success in the ever-changing sales field.

Chapter Nine

Starting the Interaction Phase

Customer interactions are useful for companies that sell goods or services to the general public, as well as for individuals who work in customer-facing positions. Because these conversations may benefit both sides, it's critical to understand the most successful methods to connect with consumers. Learning more about these client encounters may help you advance your career and grow your talents. In this chapter, we'll look at how organizations may gain from customer interactions and provide 11 recommendations for improving customer interactions.

What exactly are customer interactions?

Customer contacts include any sort of communication between a firm and a customer, whether existing or prospective. They may occur at different periods in the consumer life cycle and can be organic or planned by a corporation via marketing campaigns or sales promotions.

Customers may also begin conversations by calling or emailing a representative or messaging them via a website or social media account. Customer interactions allow the parties to strengthen their connection by establishing trust, which may help a firm get new customers or keep existing.

What steps comprise the customer contact cycle?

A customer contact cycle often has many phases, and each step is critical for both the consumer and organization. These are the stages:

Customers are in the early phases of their purchasing process at this point, and this is when they form their first impression of a firm. These clients often desire more information about what a company does and what services it offers, allowing the organization to demonstrate its value to the customer.

• **Understanding:** During this stage, a company learns about what its consumers desire by asking questions, whether via surveys, questionnaires, or in-person discussions. Having good active listening skills and the ability to sympathize with consumers will assist in ensuring success in this phase.

• **Agreeing:** At this stage, a firm turns a potential client into a current one by convincing them that the company can solve their issue. Representatives must create clear expectations about what the organization can do and give alternative ideas to assist the client in achieving their requirements.

• **Delivering:** A firm must give open communication throughout the delivery phase to ensure the consumer knows how the process works and when they can expect their product or service. This stage is critical for client retention and satisfaction.

• **Closing:** Following the completion of the purchasing process, organizations often give consumers a chance to contact them again, which might involve expressing thanks and thankfulness. This phase also aids retention by demonstrating to clients the company's commitment to continue to supply solutions.

11 methods for improving customer relations

When you work in a client-facing position, you must analyze your customer engagement approach. This may provide consistency throughout all of your customer contacts, resulting in more beneficial results for both you and your consumers. Here are 11 suggestions for improving client interactions:

1. Demonstrate empathy

Try to be compassionate with every client you contact, particularly those who have a problem or issue they want you to resolve. This might be a potential consumer looking for a new product or an existing customer who wants assistance troubleshooting the product. Listening to what they're going through and demonstrating that you understand why they feel the way they do may make them feel cared for and appreciated as a client.

2. Be open and honest.

When working in a customer-facing profession, it is critical to be open and honest with customers. If you make a mistake, you must admit it and accept full responsibility. When this happens, attempt to explain the problem, provide a genuine apology, and tell them that you are working to prevent it from happening again. Customers often want to know that you're doing everything possible to resolve the issue as soon as possible and that you know how to avoid such problems in the future.

3. Communicate across several mediums

Make it as simple as possible for consumers to communicate with you or the organization by giving assistance via many channels. You may, for example, contact them by online chat, phone, or email. Consider replying to them on the same platform where they first delivered their message to guarantee a more streamlined and efficient engagement. Furthermore, you may ensure that your consumers understand how and where to contact you if they have a problem or a worry.

4. Show your appreciation

When communicating with a consumer, strive to find methods to express your sincere gratitude. You might, for example, praise them for their patience or dedication to your firm. Making customers feel appreciated may motivate them to do business with you again in the future. It may also encourage people to share their great experiences with their friends, resulting in more traffic to the organization.

5. Use your true voice.

When conversing with consumers, instead of seeming like you're reading from a script, try speaking more truly and organically. Although it is crucial to talk professionally when attempting to address a client's problem, you may still attempt to seem as if you are not reading from a script or offering scripted comments. If a consumer approaches you for comments or sends you a message on social media, treating them as individuals might result in a more favorable and memorable connection with your customers.

6. After each consumer engagement, follow up.

Following up with each client may guarantee that they get the

assistance they need. For example, if you remedy an issue for a client, you may follow up with them in a week or two to confirm the solution is still working for them. Similarly, if you are unable to offer the assistance they need during your first engagement, you may provide them with a timetable for when they can expect to hear from you or obtain a resolution. Following up may help you give a better customer connection and experience, whether you provide a solution, feedback, or an informative resource.

7. Make use of a checklist.

While it's vital to avoid seeming like you're reading from a script, try employing a checklist during customer encounters. A checklist may assist you in ensuring that you handle every aspect of good engagement. You might want to include the following elements on your checklist:

• Make use of the customer's name.

• Inform them of your name.

• Thank you for contacting them.

• Check to see whether you grasp their statement or query.

• Inform them that you want to follow up.

• If you're communicating by email, proofread your answer.

8. Utilize customer feedback

Consider asking for consumer feedback frequently to help you enhance future encounters. A survey, for example, may assist you in detecting present or future issues. Customers may also use surveys to provide feedback about the firm, its goods and services, and the customer service experience they had. This may make them feel appreciated and provide you with specific feedback for future customer encounters.

9. Maintain your cool.

Maintain a cool approach when clients contact you with a problem or a difficulty. Approaching each client's conversation gently may help them better comprehend you and increase the effectiveness with which both sides speak and listen. Despite a potentially stressful circumstance, maintaining a cool manner will help you work together more effectively toward a solution, which can boost client satisfaction.

10. Take the initiative to discover a solution.

Although it is important to know how to tackle problems when they happen, it is as critical to predict difficulties before they occur. Being proactive and engaging clients as soon as problems develop might lead to better overall customer relationships. It might also reassure the client that you have their best interests at heart and are committed to giving the finest service possible.

11. Show your thanks to your customers.

You may express your gratitude to your consumers by providing them with a gift, a discount, corporate products, or a thank-you note. Doing so regularly demonstrates that you care about and appreciate your consumers. It may also aid in the development of an emotional connection with your clients, so increasing their loyalty and improving future customer encounters.

Here are some examples of how customer interactions may help a business:

Increased customer satisfaction and retention: Customer interactions allow you to learn about a client's demands so that you may better service them and increase their satisfaction. When a firm meets or exceeds the expectations and demands of its customers, the consumer is more inclined to do business with the company again.

• **Improved customer problem resolution:** Interactions with customers enable you to resolve any difficulties or grievances they may have. You may enhance the customer connection and let them know they can depend on you in the future by resolving client difficulties and expressing your concerns.

• **Increased client referrals:** When consumers have a good experience with a firm, they are more inclined to suggest it to others. These recommendations might result in a larger consumer base and improved revenue.

• **Improved training:** When businesses record phone conversations with customers, they may leverage the best encounters to improve training for employees. Interactions with dissatisfied clients in particular may educate team members on how to tackle similar problems on their own.

• **Stronger motivation:** Positive customer encounters may boost your morale and make you believe you're giving value to the firm. Furthermore, a commitment to producing pleasant connections might inspire you to aim for similar outcomes in the future.

Chapter ten

Getting Through the Transition Period

It takes an art to convert a prospect into a client. In most circumstances, explaining how great your product or service is and expecting payment card information is not enough. Even before the product presentation, obstacles develop during a B2B sales call.

There are several phases involved in converting prospects into consumers. This chapter teaches how to turn prospects into paying clients using numerous tactics and sales strategies.

What exactly is sales prospecting?

Prospecting is an important step in the B2B sales process. It is the process of identifying prospects (possible clients) and guiding them through a sales funnel designed to convert them into customers - while qualifying or rejecting them. A prospect is a qualified lead who has not yet been qualified as a possible buyer.

To convert prospects into consumers, do research, ask questions, and delve into a few crucial elements:

• What is the prospect's source of concern?

• Is your prospect's budget enough for your product?

• Can you provide them with the value they seek?

• Is your prospect aware of how your solution addresses their business pain points?

How to Convert Prospects to Customers

Prospect conversion might be difficult. Prospects must be qualified and fostered to be converted.

Here are nine top strategies for converting more leads into customers.

1. Recognize your prospect

Before you ever meet with the prospect for the first time, you must do some preliminary research. Take 5-10 minutes to collect information to assist you in making the best discovery call. That involves investigating the business, gatekeepers, and decision-makers on Linkedin, Google, or other tools like ZoomInfo or Lusha, and mapping them out in preparation for the discovery call.

Examine what they say and how they express it on social media. Look for prospect-written blogs and magazines. Everyone enjoys having their ego massaged. That is the first step in converting prospects into clients. Then there's the discovery call itself.

2. Improve your sales discovery call

Recognizing the various phases of a highly effective discovery call is critical for moving prospects down the funnel.

Make your inquiries strategic. You aim to establish rapport and learn about the client's needs and objectives. Learn all you can about their operational environment, competitors, requirements, and pain spots. If possible, discuss previous and existing customers who are comparable to the prospect. Explain how your solution has aided them in achieving their objectives and resolving their pain points.

Invite the prospect to the demo phase. If you like employing tried and true strategies to turn more leads into customers, here's how to enhance your SaaS discovery sales process. Even experienced salesmen should keep up to date on the newest best practices.

3. Include a FAQ section on your website.

Many prospective customers use Google to investigate solutions before speaking with a sales representative; you may assist those who seek information by including frequently asked questions (FAQ) on your website. There is no need to guess what information to provide. Instead, ask your sales, marketing, and customer service teams for the most frequently asked questions about your product.

Having a monthly sync meeting and exchanging expertise amongst these three divisions can make your sales cycles a lot smoother over time. Continue the conversation to ensure that the FAQ section is up to current, useful, and relevant.

4. Overcoming objections

Handling objections is an essential component of the sales process. The following are the two most prevalent objections:

• It's too expensive/I don't have enough money.

• I need a distinct feature.

Don't allow the objections to get in the way of your success.

• Financial concerns

A financial issue should not be used to conclude the debate. You may and should respond to criticisms in the following ways:

• Don't talk about cost until your customer realizes the value you provide.

• When a prospect objects, do not immediately drop the price. Learn more about how their finances are set up. How much money do they spend on alternatives? How much money may they save in the long run by switching to your solution? Can you save money by integrating with their existing/legacy software solutions?

• Reframe the value in terms of current expenses and cost reductions they may realize by employing your solution.

• Objections to missing features

Prospects may believe they want a certain feature, but what they really want is to address a problem. Here are a few strategies for overcoming feature-related objections:

• Inquire as to why they desire that specific functionality. You may suggest your solution if you grasp the issue they are attempting to solve.

• Recognize the advantages of the desired feature before highlighting its shortcomings.

• Explain how your program can handle the identical issue and why your solution is better.

• Highlight the extra features, cost savings, and other advantages you provide.

It goes without saying that if you can't alleviate their suffering, you should let them go. You do not want dissatisfied consumers.

5. Continue to hone your sales presentation.

There is no secret formula for creating the ideal sales presentation. Evaluate your sales process regularly, discuss your findings, and experiment with new methods to improve your sales presentation.

Here's how it's done:

• Hold frequent sales staff training sessions. What are the most frequent objections or questions they get? How do they respond? What has worked and what hasn't? You can assist them in improving their replies and arm them with the information they need after you've obtained additional insights.

• Experiment with various sales events. Organize a client webinar, a networking event, or a problem-solving hackathon for your target audience.

• Investigate the data. Which prospects, and why, are most likely to convert? When do prospects abandon the deal throughout the sales process?

• Don't get caught up with pure pitches. Spend some time listening to your prospects' worries. Keep abreast of changes influencing their sector.

• Make your pitches unique. Don't concentrate just on your attributes and what you do. Emphasize how you can help your customer address their difficulties.

6. Produce high-quality product demonstrations.

Everyone in the organization is accountable for pleasing prospects and customers. This covers the marketing and sales teams in particular since they are on the front lines and are responsible for attracting and closing prospects. You may dazzle prospects and convert them into clients by providing tailored and engaging demonstrations. The ability to deliver a customized test drive of your product demonstrates that you understand the consumer and their problems.

7. Follow up with prospects regularly.

Don't forget that prospects are people as well. They might want to buy from you, but life gets in the way. You could be one follow-up away from closing the deal. Especially when 60% of customers say "no" four times before saying "yes."

That is why emailing or calling for a quick follow-up is critical to converting more prospects. Here are three items you should include in your follow-up:

• Thank the client for their time.

• Highlight key takeaways and benefits.

• Make a strong call to action.

Not all follow-up emails are the same. However, one of the most important is the demo follow-up email. Therefore, you must get it correctly.

8. Consider your prospect's pain points.

At every opportunity, remind your prospects of their pain points and offer them a get-out-of-pain card.

When referring to the pain points, use words like "reduce", "eliminate", and "defeat". When referring to your product in this context, always follow the "you won't be wasting X amount of time/money" phrase.

9. Determine deadlines.

Giving yourself and the prospect deadlines to add mild pressure on the decision-making process is one of the greatest closing methods. The 30-day mark is an excellent opportunity to remind prospects that you will no longer be following up with them, but that you are still accessible for queries. People find it difficult to say goodbye to anything. It instills the dread of missing out. As a result, if the prospect is interested in your product, they will most likely email you back with any questions or concerns, and you can take it from there. And if they don't... well, it happens. You don't want to spend time on prospects who aren't interested in your offerings.

Chapter Eleven

Moving on to the Agreement Phase

Sales objections are a normal part of purchasing and selling, therefore even the greatest sales presenters will encounter them. As a result, becoming a successful closer requires abilities other than the presentation of product details and advantages. Strong closers must also be adept in addressing sales objections that are guaranteed to come up in a major proportion of selling attempts. To understand how to predict, discover, and successfully answer objections that will unavoidably surface during sales presentations and closing, you will require proper sales training and experience in overcoming sales objections.

What exactly is a Sales Objection?

A sales objection is a concealed or voiced worry made by a potential customer about the concept of acquiring a product or service during a salesperson's effort to sell it to the prospect. The salesperson's first task is to detect any sales obstacles that may be preventing the prospect from proceeding with the purchase. The goal is then to assist the prospect in being completely educated on all aspects of such variables, alleviating anxieties, and assisting the prospect in feeling confident in proceeding with the purchase.

Typically, sales objections are about pricing, doubt about the adequacy of the solution a product delivers to suit certain wants or desires, or missing a better offer from a vendor's competition, among others. Prospects may simply show that they have no actual interest and disregard sales representatives regardless of how good their presentations are. When this occurs, what the salesperson has encountered is not a sales objection, but rather the regrettable result of working an invalid lead.

Keeping Sales Objections to a Minimum

A combination of a well-functioning market targeting system that captures high-quality leads and an efficient lead management program that accurately classifies lead statuses and reroutes weak leads onto a lead nurturing track, rather than processing them through the direct channel of the sales pipeline toward closing, can greatly reduce the problem of finding poor leads in the hands of sales closers.

Good prospects who express genuine objections to purchasing usually do so because they do not fully comprehend the rationale for purchasing. They are, in effect, requesting more information. Once the concern is understood to be sufficiently less important than the benefits that the prospect requires/wants from the product, the prospect can feel free to proceed to become a new customer.

Identifying Objections Early in the Closing Process

Inexperienced salespeople may resort to arguing with or strong-arming prospective customers into relenting. Consumers today are usually well aware of their ability to simply walk away from a contentious sales situation or to avoid it by canceling the transaction after the fact. Wrangling to psychologically overpower prospects is thus a poor sales technique that does not contribute to the development of productive customer relationships, high closing ratios, or a larger revenue base.

Pressuring prospects to overcome objections is more likely to give the prospect the impression that your company does not truly care about their best interests and should not be trusted to behave better once they've signed a business contract. As a result, careful, consummately professional objection handling is critical to brand reputation and long-term sales success.

Sales objections are frequently more difficult to overcome after an attempt has been made to close the sale. So, before asking for the sale, work to uncover all potential objections as early as possible during the sales presentation and throughout the parallel pre-closing process.

Use pre-closing inquiries to identify possible closing impediments. Include them before the conclusion of your presentation, when you will have plenty of opportunity to discuss and ease worries. Inquire about the following:

• What are your thoughts on [identify a subject that may be confusing to the prospect]?

• Do you have any reservations about [insert possible source of concern]?

• Is there any reason why this may not work for you?

• How well do you believe this product/service will meet your needs?

• What do you believe the most important advantages would be for you?

• Do you believe the pricing is reasonable with the advantages provided by the product?

• Do you believe this has a high value for you?

How to Deal with Sales Objections

Managing sales objections, like any other business activity, is a process that, when done correctly, leads to the person performing most effectively in their function. This fundamental procedure ensures that sales closure is consistent across all company sectors. Follow these simple actions to effectively answer objections. The first four phases are just active listening steps:

• Pay close attention to understand the precise objection.

• Reiterate or repeat the prospect's worry.

• To confirm your complete comprehension of the subject, ask one or more follow-up questions.

• Recognize the prospect's legitimate worry.

• Explain to your prospect how you overcame his or her particular obstacle.

Frequently Asked Sales Questions and Answers

Most objections fall into a few broad categories: pricing or budget worries, the adequacy of the product's solution, making a spending choice or long-term contract commitment, or missing a superior offer from a rival. With enough fundamental sales training in managing client objections and experience in your sector and firm, you'll understand which objections to anticipate most often, and you'll polish your replies and handle objections more efficiently. Here are some of the most prevalent complaints and techniques for dealing with them:

• Price and Budget Issues

The cost is prohibitively expensive. This is the most common kind of sales objection. Avoid pointless debates regarding the pricing's justification. Instead, consider the product's features and total worth. Avoid lowering the price too quickly. Prospects who genuinely plan to purchase will often try to secure a discount by negotiating a lower price. Price cuts are detrimental to your company's long-term sales objectives. It erodes the perceived value of your items in your market and hurts sales and profitability.

• Our budget for this period is already fixed.

Examine the reasons why your prospect has arranged a meeting with you. Discuss the relative importance of having your product in service in their firm right now, and if it might be worthwhile to reallocate some monies earmarked for lesser priorities that may be pushed to the next budget cycle. Highlight any advantages in terms of greater efficiency, cost savings, higher revenues, and other improvements to corporate performance.

• We can't afford it right now.

Recognize that affordability might be a problem. However, address the issue of whether your product is something that the prospect's organization can genuinely afford. If the cost savings, revenue growth, and operational efficiency can justify the investment, it may make more financial sense for the organization to buy sooner rather than later. If your prospect does not have the operational funds to support a purchase of your goods, keep in touch with them until they are in a better purchasing position later on.

• Sufficiency of the Proposed Solution

We do not need your goods. The prospect's firm may not need what your product provides at this moment. However, before reaching that judgment, inquire about the department's/company's intentions and pace of development, and listen to acquire a better understanding of why your product is now seen as a low priority. If it seems that the organization does need the product, assist the prospect in understanding what it means to have the solution today, as well as the expected degree of positive influence on their business performance.

• **Your product lacks a required feature or is incompatible with our systems.**

Your company's product isn't always the best match. However, depending on the age and effectiveness of the prospect's present product(s), they may be better off replacing them with yours. It may also be worthwhile for them to implement a method to make your product operate inside their system. Before you decide to write off the lead, ask questions to establish how much value their current product is producing for them.

• **We are pleased with the product/service we are currently utilizing.**

Many busy individuals would prefer to live with inconvenience than go through the process of even little change. Recognize how wonderful and crucial it is to be pleased with the things and services you use. Still, think about why the prospect decided to meet with you about your offering. Before going on, discuss the kind of needs/challenges that may be relevant to the prospect and assess whether or not there is anything you can do to assist.

• I have heard some negative things about your firm.

Make no attempt to defend yourself or your organization. Instead, just thank the prospect for providing the information and offer to share it with your management. If applicable, mention the number of pleased consumers your organization serves, or another noteworthy performance metric. Then, go on to talk about the worth of your product, its major features, its great advantages, and the many reasons why so many people have become such devoted customers and have recommended so many friends and acquaintances to your company.

Provide the prospect with an amazing experience while working with you to change their perception and encourage them to switch from posting negative remarks to making more positive comments about your organization.

• Making a Financial Decision

I refuse to sign a contract. If the prospect seems to want to use your product but is hesitant to commit to the length of time necessary by your company's normal contract, check if a modified agreement can be struck to allow for a shorter term of commitment. If that isn't a possibility, acknowledge that no one likes contracts and explain to the prospect that the contract defends their interests, defines their rights, outlines precisely what has been promised to them, and indicates the boundaries of their commitment.

• **This is not something I can sell to top management.**

Inquire about the decision-makers name and contact information, as well as the name and contact information of their gatekeeper(s). Prepare for the arguments that your prospect is likely to raise, and offer them with a strong set of facts to back up the major advantages your solution will bring. Then, while you're still in the prospect's office, attempt to organize a meeting with the decision-maker to maximize referral leverage.

• **I'm too busy right now to deal with this.**

Request that the prospect reschedule a meeting with you at a later date. If a new date is not available at this time, follow up with the prospect regularly, give them some useful products to continue being helpful and establishing rapport, and attempt again to reschedule when suitable.

• Better Competition Offer

We use a different provider. There is no need to persuade this prospect since they have already identified a need for the kind of service your organization provides. Inquire about the performance of their existing vendor's product and service. Take note of any challenges that your product can address for them. Compare the characteristics and advantages of the two rival items and demonstrate your offering's overall higher value. If the prospect is under contract with the existing vendor, see if you can give a discount to cover the expense of terminating the deal.

• I'd want to go shopping.

Say you like the possibility of thinking in that manner. Recognize that a well-informed consumer is by far the best for your business. Explain that, thankfully, you can assist the prospect in saving a significant amount of time and resources on comparisons. Explain that it is your responsibility to be completely acquainted with what is offered in this specific category of product/service. Display the comparisons that differentiate your product and demonstrate how it provides the greatest value to purchasers.

• We can get it cheaper somewhere else.

Some prospects try to decrease the selling price by claiming to be aware of a rival that sells the same product at a cheaper price. First, determine if cheaper costs for a similar product are available on the market. Discuss the distinctions between price and cost, as well as price and value. Concentrate on the features and advantages that result in higher cost savings, increased efficiency, and other quantifiable consequences that raise the value of your product.

• Objections that are not specified

I'd want to think about it. This is not a complaint. It's a prelude to a genuine objection. So, ask the prospect what he or she wants to think about explicitly. Respond to the prospect's objection once he or she has stated it.

If the prospect is unsure about which precise questions to consider, say, "Why don't you think about it while I'm here with you, so I can answer any questions you may have while you're thinking about it?" Inform the prospect that you will take a break and give him/her some time to think about it right now." Encourage him/her to take as much time as is necessary, and promise them that you'll simply be in the next room, ready to answer any questions they may have while you're still there to explain everything.

• What is your refund policy?

Seasoned sales professionals understand that this seemingly benign inquiry conceals much more. It refers to the prospect's true degree of commitment and is a red sign warning that your deal will be jeopardized after you've done all possible to close it. You'll be better off without a sale, retaining the prospect connection for potential later close, than putting yourself and the prospect through a deceptive conversion process that is unlikely to last the duration of the scheduled cancelation time.

Address this issue as an objection rather than just responding that the cancellation period is three or seven days, for example. Understand the significance of not proceeding with the formal agreement when the prospect is at ease with the idea of canceling. Discuss the significance of being committed to the choice and concentrating on the tremendous advantages of the product/service and all that having it will mean to the prospect.

Viewpoint on Responding to Sales Objections

The frequency of contacts with prospects who have not been adequately qualified is reduced to a bare minimum with correctly focused marketing and expertly handled leads. Nonetheless, sales objections will always be an expected part of the sales process. Many are surmountable with the use of sophisticated sales training, roleplaying, and professional experience.

However, there are occasions when you should walk away. You'll leave your contact information and a lot of goodwill for the prospect. You will have made a new business friend with someone who may eventually become a happy new client, or who may at the very least share good word of mouth about their experience with your firm.

Remember that the path to excellent sales success is rather straightforward: provide a high-value product, work good leads, provide a solid presentation, assist prospects in working through objections, and reclose after addressing objections. Consider not feeling defeated if you do not convert every single prospect, but rather bringing on as many as possible as new clients.

Overarching these basics, bear in mind the Harvard Business Review's opinion on the quality route to sales success: "Instead of focusing solely on revenue, salespeople should concentrate more on helping buyers accomplish their goals."

Chapter Twelve

Taking Business Connections to New Heights

In the fast-paced world of business, where transactions often take priority, the importance of developing long-term relationships with customers cannot be stressed. While sealing a contract may provide immediate benefits, developing long-term relationships is the fundamental basis for long-term success. In this chapter, we will discuss the critical necessity of cultivating long-term relationships versus transactional commerce and how every person in the company is responsible for nurturing and maintaining these priceless ties.

• Aside from Transactions:

Transactional business partnerships are driven by a single transaction of products or services and concentrate on short-term rewards. Building long-term connections, on the other hand, transcends the limitations of a single transaction. It entails knowing the client's specific demands, adjusting to their changing wants, and being a trusted partner rather than a simple service supplier.

• Loyalty and trust:

Trust is the foundation of every lasting relationship. Clients are more willing to commit to long-term relationships when they believe a company will constantly give value. Building trust cultivates customer loyalty, laying the groundwork for repeat business, recommendations, and a favorable reputation that may extend beyond the original client base.

• Customer Experience from Every Angle:

Long-term ties allow companies to give a more comprehensive consumer experience. Organizations may personalize their offers and services to better match the client's requirements by studying their history, preferences, and issues. This individualized approach improves the whole customer experience, enhancing the client's attachment to the company.

• Mutual Development:

Long-term connections are beneficial to both the customer and the company. As the demands of the customer change, the company may alter its goods or services appropriately. This response not only indicates a dedication to the client's achievement, but it also presents the company as a partner in their road to success.

Everyone Contributes:

Long-term customer relationships are not only the duty of the sales team; they are the result of a collaborative effort involving all departments within a firm. Each person contributes to the client experience, from customer service and marketing to product development and leadership. A great, seamless experience requires alignment throughout the whole enterprise.

• Communication that works:

Open and honest communication is critical to long-term success. Client connections. Clients understand that they are more than simply a transaction when they get regular check-ins, information on new offers, and a readiness to resolve problems. Effective communication fosters rapport, comprehension, and a feeling of collaboration.

• Problem Solving and Flexibility:

No partnership is without difficulties. Long-term relationships are strengthened not by avoiding issues, but by dealing with them quickly and efficiently. Clients like organizations that show flexibility and dedication to addressing challenges cooperatively, which reinforces the client's trust in the relationship.

• Positive Workplace Culture:

A client's experience is not limited to conversations with a sales professional; it includes every point of contact with the business. A good business culture in which workers are aligned with client-centric ideas improves the entire client experience. Clients can tell when a company prioritizes their requirements, leaving an indelible impression.

Conclusion

Every salesperson faces challenges like competition, limited time, and lack of customer response. To overcome these, you should analyze competition, evaluate your advantages, and use tools like sales reports, profile enrichment technology, and automation solutions. You should also negotiate with prospects, handle rejection, and handle criticism. Sales is a fulfilling profession that requires integrity, commitment to value, and genuine concern for helping others. To improve customer experience, organizations should adopt a customer-centric strategy, cultivate a customer-focused culture, improve data quality, and consider long-term relationships.

Effective questioning strategies, understanding customer pain areas, and balancing sales goals are essential. Customer interactions are crucial for gaining trust, answering inquiries, and providing products or services. Companies should show empathy, be truthful, use various communication channels, express gratitude, follow up, use checklists, solicit customer input, maintain composure, anticipate issues, and express gratitude.

Sales prospecting involves identifying potential customers, building connections, providing FAQs, and addressing financial concerns. Regular evaluation of the sales process, training workshops, and product demos can minimize objections. Active listening techniques and engaging prospects in productive ways can help overcome obstacles. Sales success depends on offering high-value products, generating quality leads, and fostering long-term partnerships.